SCARS

SCARS

by

BRYN GRIFFITHS

LONDON
J. M. DENT & SONS LTD

FOR DAVID AND BARTLEY

CONTENTS

ACKNOWLEDGMENTS

Acknowledgments are due to the following publications, where many of these poems have appeared:

> *The Listener*
> *Poetry Wales*
> *Poetry Review*
> *London Welshman*
> *Transatlantic Review*
> *Tribune*

Acknowledgments are also due to the B.B.C. Third Programme, Rediffusion Television, and Television Wales and the West for the poem on Aberfan, which they commissioned.

EXILES

The blue stones stand, ring within silent ring,
in the worn centre of Stonehenge,
the centre of the land itself.
Blue stones,
hewn from far Caermeini, you crossed
moor and mountain, the sea's crushing road,
towards the ageless sanctity of this wide plain
where winds have hammered you,
century
after
century . . .

And here, under the sun's slow wheel,
the blond grass still rolls like a windy sea
across a kinder landscape
than the western one you once knew.

You became blunt alien cogs in the stone clock
of the centuries. You are forever strangers here.

But you can never return, toll back the past,
regain your former shape of being. Always,

it seems, you must stand here,
worn by weather and the marching years,
your granite roots groping towards infinity.
Time has no meaning for you:
year
after
year
the tourists, the strangers, climb
your scarred sides and wonder at your meaning—

not understanding your difference from the others,
not for one moment comprehending
the reason in your being so far from home.

You stand apart in your squat stature and
true difference: you are forever strangers here.

[1]

CLOS-Y-GRAIG

There we were happy and,
it seemed, safe for a short hour,
huddled in the hollow of the rock
that climbed above autumn
landscapes more radiant
than any seen before.

There, light years away from
the endless blast of the city,
we could play at being people.
Farmers, postmen, ministers
and bards called, and stayed,
and passed the time of day away.

They had time for people.

But our fleeting days there,
in the far hills, were soon gone,
and life pressed down again.

Why did we have to return here?

SAFARI

I try to track her now through darkness,
the shadowed jungle of an old despair,
but she escaped too well, killing our brief affair
with one swift strike towards sanity.

I came upon her suddenly, predatory as ever,
and for a time shackled her with tenuous ties
which I, this day, find no less binding: I pace,
endlessly, caught in the dark cage of my skull.

Seeking at last a freedom from my searching flesh,
she fled through the stone forests of Europe
where my hunting fingers could not blindly grope
in search of her and fading memory.

And these days, held back by harsh bars of distance,
I map the darkness with her spun beauty of hair—
crouched dumb like a beast in the mind's still lair—
remembering a cloud of gold bright against the night.

Strange that I, hunter become the hunted,
should track her through life and passing youth
as she smiles, sighs, breathes in another's mouth—
my love now lost in clawing tangles of cold words!

Behind the memoried blue beasthood of her eyes—
behind the white frontiers of placid bone—
there clicks a brain of living stone
which still beats at me across the miles of sea

and forest that separate and eternally divide.
And yet, within safe distance, I once caught
the wildness of her flesh as she fought
to free herself from her body's need for me.

I hear again her voice, clear as a hunting yell,
and the anguish in her groan of sudden pain—
the soft surrender of woman crying for love again—
as I search for her in the slow safari of my life.

ACCIDENT

Wheeling clear of the dangerous bend,
slowing, accelerating,
slowing again,
my eyes
caught the obscene collage
of the smashed and crumpled car:
just an agony of metal stoning
the road:
blind headlamps staring skywards:
bodies burst like old rag dolls:
blood, stagnant as marsh mud, and
thick coils
of clustered entrails
falling
from the ripped flesh
into the hard dust of the road.
A crowd had suddenly, bloodily,
gathered,
like a sullen cloud of flies
converging on a crack-backed beetle.
One man stepped forward,
shoved a shining
black shoe into the slow red flood,
and said, with stunned wonder,
'It's blood'.
His interest dimmed when, wiping
his shoe on the road's grassed verge,
he found a stain remained
that
no polishing would remove.
Someone had telephoned, and suddenly
a cavalcade
of ambulances
and police cars screamed black and white
and black and white around the bend.

                    'All dead,'
         the uniformed men said, tugging
         at torn bodies, fenders, buckled
         wheels, until the tangled flesh fell
                   soddenly into summer dust.
         I drove on, braking carefully
         at traffic lights, seeing the sudden
         rain congeal like blood
                             beyond
         my windscreen,
                        above my head.

ABERFAN

An Elegy for the Children of Aberfan

We have come to October again, autumn, the slow dying
of the year that takes the mind back into memory.
The worn clock of the seasons has wound down,
and the shadowed hands of Time now point
towards that other autumn when the children,
the many, many children, died at Aberfan.

Into that last dark, then, they went to die,
one with the vast company of the dead,
caught in the black flood that smashed
the morning's melody, to slaughter a child's innocence,
in the shadowed valley
from which all song and sanity soon fled.

All the haunting, midnight fears of childhood,
all mankind's ancient fear of nature's rage,
came alive after long years lying in wait—
came alive in the mask of coaldust man had made—
to leave the living with their bleak heritage
of loss . . . of hiraeth . . . and of hate.

Some speak of a certain dignity in death—
but death is not dignified when children die!

Down the valleys, then, went the cold word of death.
Cottage after cottage fell silent
with the echoing knowledge of new disaster—
the children paying, life for life
the final price of the fathers' labour—
and then fury and question burned anew under

The drumming skies of Wales—the old, old question
on the root, the cause, and the why of it all!

All over the world the children were dying—
in Arabia, the Americas, Africa and Asia—
but the world was a far place—too far
to comprehend for those whose worlds
lay lost below the slurried flood of death.

Into that last dark they went to die,
singing yet again of Heaven's simple bread,
praising God in the morning psalms of childhood
as the debris of decades moved, shuddered,
and swept down the mountain to crush
the school where once the word of God was said.

But God had no place here in those first hours,
he seemed but memory in that broken landscape . . .
only his word lingered on, echoing
like a dying song in the minds of men,
and the tomb's silence of deserted chapels.

We could not voice our agony then,
the soundless terror of day made night,
the fear for the children caught in seconds
by the darkness, driving out of darkness,
that made a mockery of the day's bright light.

The children died, together at the last,
unaware of coming dissent and argument,
struck down by nightmare born of the past.
They died because we, drugged with inertia,
blindly accepted a heritage of guilt . . .
and questioned nothing.

[6]

But all over the world the children were dying—
burnt by the bestial scorch of napalm;
wasted by disease on disease;
starving to small skeletons in famine after famine;
scattered like autumn leaves by the winds of history.

In that time of tragedy all worked together—
to save the present, to undo the past—
where so many lost futures lay in that last common bed.
And then later, aware of guilt, we blamed, accused,
denied and claimed, while other, distant voices
sang with blinding love for the living and the dead.

Some forget too soon the memory of a child.
Aberfan will stir, and live, and grow again:
the new cottages, schools and memorials, will climb
the scarred hillsides and leave the past behind. . . .
But money is nothing, dry dust in the wind,
and this cannot compensate the death of a child.

We have known death too well in Wales:
it shadows our songs, our poetry, our lives.
We have walked all our days with death,
And we have known its many brutal ways—
but never such a death of innocence as this!

Into that last dark they went to die,
buried by the debris of another day,
while in Africa and Asia, below brilliant skies,
other children drifted towards another night—
eyes dimmed by disease to the loss of sight—

their green worlds fading to a final darkness
under the siege of blindness and the body's slow decay.

Some forget too soon the memory of children
we have seen buried, blinded, burning to death
across the front pages of newspapers . . .
we have been silent, year after year,
while the hollow voices of our time have clamoured
loudly, making headlines, achieving nothing.

[7]

And still the wars rage on, the children die,
and death runs wild under sky and sky and sky.

We have been silent for too long: now we know
where the blame lies . . . from Aberfan to Vietnam . . .
for all over the world the children are dying—
burning to ashes in Vietnam's obscenity of slaughter;
crucified in the African massacres by brute fear and hate;
wasting to death in the senseless famines of India.

Wars, disasters, fire and famine kill the children . . .
and the knowledge of death and guilt of apathy are ours.

The children are dying, in the far places of the Earth,
but for us, in Wales, Aberfan
has become our symbol of the endless folly,
the useless sacrifice,
and the eternal agony and tragedy of man.

We could not voice our pity then,
the vast compassion of a world in dread,
stunned by the shock of unthinkable tragedy,
and only now, in knowledge of light lost forever,
can we sing of our blind love for the living and the dead.

KINGFISHER

> The shadowed dingle,
> cool and singing as a chapel,
> hushed its summer melody
> into a waiting silence
> for what song of flight
> only the woodland knew:
> and then, breaking the silence,
> burning out of shadow,
> a shard of rainbow

splintered the dark air
to become, in sunlight,
the kingfisher
in whistling flight.
Caught in this green cage
of whispering leaves,
the gigantic glade
of a child's green memory,
the bird broke open for me
childhood's time-locked book
of half-forgotten memories—
each blurring beat
of its wings turning back
the pages of the years
until again I stood here,
seeing with first wonder
the sun's colours caught
in a bullet of bright feathers
flashing down the dingle
to where the stream
turned calm. The lost world
of childhood lived but
brief seconds, clear as
the first summer mornings,
and then the kingfisher
had gone, back into shadow,
and the full book
of my days closed again
on still space—
the pang of known beauty
dying again into memory
with that airborne
brilliance of a bird!

ON THE DOLE

He stood by the bar,
squat, flat-capped, still strong
at fifty but condemned to
the scrapheap of industry's waste.
A miner on the dole,
with nowhere to go,
the blue scars of his trade—
a network of harsh memory—
still mapping his past of pain.

Most of his generation
went coughing into retirement,
but he had ten good years to go.

He stood by the bar,
a long lingered over pint
clamped between fingers
the size of small spades,
counting his small change and
the gray days dwindling
into the empty future.
Thirty-five toiling years
have come, at last, to nothing;

his strength no match
for machines, his mind
outclassed by computers.

WORLD MAKER

(for Martyn Teifion)

My son, now you fill our days
with wonder at your small cries,
the first smiles, the awakening ways
of your young life. We map out
a rich world of living for you—
and yet your destiny is a mystery
clenched in Time's vast hand.
You have brought us new happiness,
you bless our days with a bright presence,
but we know, too, the shadows
and fears of your thousand futures,
still forming, still filing into infinity.

What will you be, my son,
what far universes will you see?

World maker, life shaper, you link
untold generations in eternity's chain
and hold the future within you yet again.

KESTREL

Drifting inland, ploughing the wide
acres of empty air,
    the kestrel
trawls the coastal landscape
with his hunting eyes,
pinions piercing air,
until a prey breaks from the cover
of woodland shadows—
     to bring down
the kestrel in killing flight!

The furred innocence of the woods
buckles below the smashing blow
of beak and talon, dies,
as the dappled destroyer
of the air drives in to kill.
           It is over here,
killing is done, but elsewhere,
in jungle, desert, or granite pass,
under the distant sights
of a sniper's rifle,
           a man
steps from shadow into sunlight
into shadow as a human hawk
coldly strikes his blithe kill
to earth which has known
the blood of centuries.
           The kestrel,
hungered and rooting
in the broken body of its kill,
is working out blind destiny—
driven by the blood's code
of nature and necessity—
while man, idly booting
           the broken
obscenity of blood and bone,
is less than man, is below
the predatory bird,
in his knowing bestiality.

JUST A TRADE

Ianto, the undertaker, enjoys his trade.
He is a skilled mechanic of death, adept
at preserving the stilled machinery
of the flesh.
       'It's just a trade,' he says,
'and a lonely one at that—
with nothing but corpses for company!'

But there are compensations, as Ianto admits,
and one of them lies in the work itself.
He works with an icy pride, embalms
dead friend and foe alike, for old feuds
are forgotten here; nothing matters any more.

RECLAMATION

       They are trying to reclaim
the shattered floor of the valley
which men once tore apart, years ago,
before our time.
       They are trying
to erase the stain of the past,
to seed earth soured by a century
of slag and sulphur fumes,
to heal the cankered sore that
is today Landore.
       They may succeed,
and the valley may one day
be green again, but we cannot forget
the men who turned a vale
of woodland, meadow and clear streams

into a waste of ash littered
with the debris of forgotten industry—
the long dead men who fouled
this once green world of Wales!
                    We can but look
forward to the coming of green
and watch for the new destroyers.

REMEMBERING

Remember the winter night we met,
you unknowing, I unfree, alone
in that tame Bayswater party—

I drown now in your torrent of hair—

while outside, in the London night,
it was raining and the slick wet
pavements shone back blackly at a sky

in which stray planes groaned through
endless cloud towards horizons
blurring to the haze of infinity—

*and still, cariad, your voice calls
in soft cries which splinter air—*

and I remember the later hours
when we lay silent before beginning
the first tremor which presages love—

*movement which triggers cool sweat
on the soft white flesh you bare—*

a transient love which ran its
course from the rocking room in
Bayswater to Kensington to Swansea,

in fading autumn, when again we lay
listening to the sky fall, flooding
the wide nightscapes of Wales—

your thighs cling, your eyes flare—

while all the night long far cars
whispered by on the wet roads
which ran through the drowned land—

our eyes lock in one blind stare—

and then we moved on, towards
the ending of another journey,
to the western edge of Wales

where, one sun-blessed morning,
we awoke to a knowledge of love
beginning to fade in the new day—

*to break free, yet unfree, in cold
sunlight crashing from nowhere—*

with a new warmth kindling from
the ashes of the past fire of flesh
remembered in the long return—

*your sunlight breaking again echoes
the last autumn colours of radiant air—*

driving through the countryside's
vast silence breaking to first light,
so that we could lie again like this,

moving slowly in the easy patterns
of a practised love, coming full circle,
to love in this last London night—

our flesh fused without care!

SON UNKNOWN

Son, unknown to me, lost
in my uncaring youth,
how tall do you stand now?
Does your hair fall fair,
widow-peaked, like mine
as a book-loving lonely child?
Are your eyes my eyes?

Questions, questions,
all my days as I picture you
in a thousand ways,
growing to manhood, never
knowing me in my grief
for what is past and gone—
the blind seeds sown in youth.

Son unknown to me, lost to me,
where do you walk now?

SCARS

Here there are scars—
               and here,
here, here, and here.

Below breast, unseen, marking
the heart, fissuring belly,
              visible
as green, livid as old agony
in the groin,
reminding muscles of past pain.

And here there are scars—
black in the mind's black vault—
blasting through the eyes'
wide gunports in broadside

after soundless broadside.

Feel my forehead where thoughts
have carved the flesh.

Life marks mark me. I am one scar—
but a million others
                    scar
the city streets.

Only the young, the smooth young,
are free of such signatures.

We scar the one blue-green planet.
We, mankind, mark meadow,
mountain, plain and valley—
                    cloud
the seas and skies
with the drifting debris
of the generations.

Soon we will scar the far planets
with our presence—
while our world hurtles on
through silent spaces—
                    but
here, visible, there are scars.

THIS MIGHT FALL

This might fall—
fall in ten thousand
distintegrating bricks
in which I will lie a mess
of blood and bone in the mass
of debris—fall one night
when I lie asleep with you, my love,
or you, or you, or you—
and not know anything.

'It might fall,' said
my surveyor friend on his
first visit, 'the angle is extreme.'

Warnings, warnings,
year after year—
but I live here in this
white lighthouse of a house
leaning down Hampstead Hill.

This might fall—
and you might be here then, my love,
or you, or you, or you—
and we will be really mixed up
in the mass of debris.
But I live here . . . and I like
to live dangerously.

THE DEATH OF DUFFRYN RHONDDA

(for the miners of Duffryn Rhondda)

The colliery has closed this day,
bringing to a bleak end the long years
in the lamp-starred darkness,
and the miners now wander blindly
into another darkness of despair.

(There is no other work or future here.)

They will stand at street corners again,
telling of old friends and the dead days
forever gone into buried memory,
and they will know, forty years later,
a new depression, born of progress,
settling to slag the mind's
worn landscape with familiar despair.
But still they will sing,
the flashing wit melting into one
with the sudden shafts of autumn sunlight,
knowing of the close comradeship
which has always been theirs.

Each generation has lived this way.

Rooted in the valley's torn landscape,
part of its joy and blue-scarred pain,
the miners here have worked out
their harsh days in a long cycle
of singing, suffering, and death—
a slowly wheeling dream of light and shadow—
that is one with the gray past
and this turbulent century's
packed hoard of memories.

Fortunes were made here, sweated
from men who tore the black fruit from
the earth's blind womb with bleeding hands
and even their children, stunted
by depression and disaster,
grew up with the sour taste
of coaldust thick on their lips . . .
But the mine-owners, living well
in the green lands or distant London,
could not even imagine the vast darkness
of the mines and the depths
of agony suffered there.

They reaped a rich harvest then,
building their opulent mansions,
counting profits like milestones in a march
towards some summit of coveted wealth
that could never be reached,

for their greed was too great.

And all this was done at a safe distance,
out of sight of mine and poverty.
They made their fortunes and left,
leaving the butchered valleys
to linger on in the slow oblivion of decay.
They are gone but the miners remain.
And above these men, in these quiet days,
through morning mist and sunlight,
the new fir trees creep across the bald hills
like a deep green cancer—to obscure
the past until emptiness reigns, the cycle ends,
and the wheel comes full circle at last.

They will stand at street corners again,

knowing no other way of life,
and their bewildered questions
will endlessly accuse those who made
their distant decisions coldly, economically,

without thought for men scrapped before
their time. Morgan, Idwal, Meirion
where will you go? When will you work again,
be whole men again, sing your songs again,
for you know no other way of life?

The planners, the economists, put forward
their cold figures and theorize;
but they know nothing of your experience—
your singing Saturdays, your history of tragedy,
your blunt but true humanity.
They live by other rules: statistics
stun them with arid beauty: the graphs
of production and rising costs
are not counted against the smashed bodies,
the mine-widowed women,
and the lungs of men slowly turning
to stone with each new layer of dust.

The Depression crouched here like
a great beast, sucking the spirit like blood
from a battered people, but still
they survived and lived on through
the Depression, war and peace,

and the final passing of the mine-owners.

But then a Labour Government came,
loaded with promise, fat with empty praise,
to kill this scarred valley at last.
Their party was born in these valleys,
built on the loyalty of men like miners,
but the time for loyalty seems past.
And yet these men wore out their buckled bodies here,
coughed up their splintering lungs
in a filthy blend of blood and dust;
they toiled under the piled strata
of stressed rock, moving towards a vague future,
certain only of the earth's presence
and a crushing death waiting long years to strike.

The time for loyalty seems past,

the miners are redundant, finished,
and the Duffryn dies as the statistics say it must.
And they will stand at street corners again,
telling of the lost years and the '26 strike,
caged in a forty-year-old living dream of the past.

SNAKES

Only islands, such as Ireland,
they say, are free of such silent
tyranny of writhing life. The chill
eyes, the flickering tongue
flashing fluidly between lips hard
and ridged as those of an aged crone,
hold the careful watcher rooted
for long eternal seconds
till surprise is past. But here,
in this burnt land, the coil
and slow slam of the snake
into the round eye which punctures
the packed earth speaks
of the Pacific where the women
thread sleek bunching sinew
into pulsing purses of flesh—
speaks also of the Roman women—
sucking jaws eating the blind heads—
who drew down on the tamed fury
which drilled towards anguish.
How could melanesian and vestal
accept such cold movement
in the ripe sac of the body?
No words can signal sound
into shapes of meaning
and inform us of cause and reason.

Only desert, jungle, and long
dead temple can now tell
of the appled Eden where a snake
spelt out the naked sin and
the first wrong which lay in words.

LIFE AFTER DEATH

'Life after death?' he repeated,
'there's no such thing, mun,
I've been in this game long enough
to know all about that!'
Ianto seemed sure of himself,
speaking from strength,
but I persevered. 'There *could* be,'
I argued, 'after all,
there are such things as ghosts,
and spirits, and things like that.'
'I don't believe in them,'
he said, now dogmatic
and certain in his stand, 'after all—
who ever came *back* from the dead?
No one ever did!'
'Jesus Christ,' I suggested.
'History has it that he
was resurrected from the dead . . .'
'Don't believe in him either,'
he replied, 'it's just a lot
of old myth and legend, mun.'
'But it's *history*,' I persisted.
'History is bunk, boy,' he said,
echoing Ford. 'If you'd been
an undertaker long as I have,
you'd know there's only *death*
after death; nothing more than that.'

A NEW ADHESIVE

'They've got a new napalm now.'
'Oh, I see, but what's so different about it?'
'It sticks.'
'Sticks?'
'Yes, it sticks—to flesh.'
'What kind of flesh?'
'Oh, Vietcong, North Vietnamese . . .'
'It's a selective napalm then . . .'
'Well, I wouldn't say *selective*—
a few women and kids get caught sometimes—
but, you know, accidents happen.'
'Yes . . . I suppose they should have
stayed in their paddy fields.'
'You're dead right there!'
'It must burn like hell . . .'
'It does. That's the beauty of it!
This new stuff is *really* adhesive.'
'That's what I like about Americans—
they're so bloody efficient!'

SCARRED LANDSCAPE

This is the scarred land where the soil
is scorched almost beyond recall.
This is the valley of the Tawe where a river
the colour of rust gropes through black banks
of slag towards a sea fouled, as always, by man.

Strangers ruined this landscape. Their greed
made the first metal industry here flourish;
packed the harbour, quay to quay,
with Horn-weathered windjammers; brought
a million tons of copper to flow—
a blinding river of liquid wealth—
from glowing furnace after furnace.

But the strangers never settled here,
near the smoking desert of their making;
they preferred the gracious living
and the softer landscapes of England.
They came just to rape a timeless beauty;
to warp and buckle men with breaking toil;
to make money and leave to loot elsewhere . . .

They are long gone, just shadows in history,
but their marks remain, scarring the land,
to remind us of the past again and again.

BUS STOP

'Till the bus stops,' she said, 'don't get off.'
And then she added: 'It's dangerous, you see.'
I smiled and said, 'All right; don't worry.'
She seemed uncertain. 'But I do worry, you see'—
She took a fare—'you might fall'—
Her hands plucked at hair—'might break your neck.'
She looked strangely hopeful. 'I won't,' I said.
The bus was slowing now; I poised.
'Could lose my job,' she argued, 'if you get hurt.
Please . . . till the bus stops!' But I jumped off,
Missed the stop, and landed here amongst strange faces.
'Hello,' I said to the faces, and smiled uncertainly.
'Hello,' they chorused back, and then, collectively,
'How's things?' I stalled, remembering the 'Goodbye!'
The conductress callously screamed after me.

DEATHLOVE

Ianto loves the dead.
He smiles a bland loving smile
as he works, and Llew
and Sian and Bran
smile blankly back at him.

Only he, he insists, *understands*.
Only he can hear
the soundless detonations
in the dead flesh vibrating
beneath his sonar touch.

To watch his thick fingers
on the splayed female bodies,
caressing the cold curve
of thigh and belly,
is to understand the locked

hunger that lives in him.
Only time, the years' grin
which drills his face, tells
of the packed charge of his senses
building towards a strange catharsis.

GREEN DREAMS

Sometimes, in summer, the woods dream for me
in the day's long melody of sun and flowers.
At dusk, when the sun dies, the woodland
becomes a world of strangeness where shadows
throng and follow till I stand still for fear.
I fear the clenching flowers that devour;
the green fangs of grass biting through dank soil;
the stealthy trees that freeze to sudden stillness
at the eye's warning scream of impossible movement.

It was here, in childhood, that I buried
my dark hoard of fears out of the mind's clear sight.
Did they take root here, to spawn a thousand terrors,
to pack the earth with fear for my return?
I stand still, and listen, but nothing moves.
Only a vast silence thrives and hymns
through shadowed chapels of oak and elm as
the day dies and night comes alive to thunder
like childhood thought through these waiting glades.

TRIAD

I

The making began in the dead summer
When we listened for bells to ring below
The sea: the drowned cantref where Seithenin
Once sang away his ebbing life under
The crash of falling walls and tumbling tides
Where now the lost and legend past collides
With the present and begins to founder
Under Time's flood: this was a beginning,
The fusing of the future, and the slow
Charge burns on in us and in our prisoner.

Through a round space the blind cells spun,
Coiling like star clouds in a closed universe,
While the bells tolled away our love's quiet hour.

II

I see the seed gather in its darkness,
Growing towards the blood-packed charge of bone
And sinew which ticks away the clock-slow,
Season-slow, hours of a shaping year:
Death begins at the first detonation
Of light on eyes, and its celebration
Sings of the long cycle of faith and fear
And our lives passing in the shadow-show
Which shackles man in his knowledge alone
In a universe where only words bless.

And I know, for the first time, unique fear
Dancing cold in the vast locked ballroom
Of the brain—a ghostly waltz of shadow with shadow—
And a new darkness falling sudden as April rain.

III

Spectral hands have set the heart's clock beating,
Twin pendulums shudder the locking flesh,
And life rages in the bone-barred hollow—
Building to break from the time-vault of night—
Where the fast blood blasts down the corridor
Of the body's prison: the inheritor
Grows towards grief, the first knowledge of light
Which is the first sorrow, and we must follow
The progress of pain as the clenched hands thresh
In the dumb fury that is our making.

We see again the tides seeding the soil with salt,
The bells chiming away the centuries in seconds,
The making of myth in one thunderous hour.

IV

And part of me now lives in another.
I move in the slow tensing flesh under
The white breast and the thrumming sinews stressed
To an arrowed flight from bone. This is pain—
The mind's rainbow of bright splintering colour—
And only the woman knows its clamour
As the shackled stranger begins to strain
And break through to blinding light the haired crest,
The brilliant eyes awake with first wonder,
The life alone and like no other.

And still the creatures of the sea wind their way
Through the vast silence of drowned churches
Where liquid hands toll the bells of the waterclock:
And the bells toll for you and me and you and me.

V

The time-bomb of the body bursts and sings
Of our triad love and the summer days
When we made another to know our pain:
Two worlds meet in the maelstrom of the blood's
Blending—and love is born again in Wales:
This is the inheritor: he gales
The green world of the sunlit room with floods
Of sound to tell us that we live again:
He tells us of present truth, of past praise,
Made clear by birth breaking like white wings.

*Out of the drumming darkness, ghosting the day
With reality, the child joins the players and the play:
And he, too, is legend: one link a timeless chain.*

VI

My blind sensing tells of the living shell
Which has sung for me these long years—
The body's conch that calls from another room
Where green seas swing still around a tide-tolled bell.
The final hour has come, renewing old fears,
For flesh has been freed from the catacomb
To bring our destiny home where it fell
In a bright welter of life. And who hears
The child's clamour echoed in the womb,
And the thunder of death in its crying knell?

*We have come to the ancient knowledge at last,
Knowing we are triad, part of the past,
And yet one with the new generations
That march in us through all our days.*

GROWING

You see, my love, how your body
blossoms into spring; building bone
and small sinews in the round flesh
which I have held close
and cherished for so many
long nights.
       Summer brought to being
your body's beauty, and only you
and I, and the wheeling months,
have seen a night's splendour grow
towards the fruition of other life.
       You string sinews
in a small universe; stud a skull
with bright buds of eyes;
branch bone into the coiled life
which waits through long months—
beating slow under the coded
command of countless ages—
beating till
       the blinding blade
of birthlight! My love roots
in you, drawing strength
to bear the harvesting light,
and you count the waiting days as I
gentle and garden all your whims
and new ways
       through your slowly
falling hours. And you will see,
my love, the flesh break as
you grow for me, you come to me,
you meet my mouth and flower!

'But I *love* Wales and the Welsh,'
said the Englishman, said the Englishman,
said the Englishman—buying up
cottage after cottage, farm after farm,
until the entire countryside
smacked of flat English shires.
Even the vowels, here, were now flat.
Entire villages—now, of course,
redecorated—have become
dormitories for Birmingham.

And the young married farmhand
seeking a house—a home?
Well he couldn't compete
with the moneybags from Manchester
who wanted to play farmer . . .
And then, holiday cottages were in demand.

So each year the Englishman came
to spend a few summer days in Wales.
And each year he wondered
why the natives—strange,
but loveable people—seemed less.

And this is all, cariad, day following night
in one drifting dream of living,
and this state of blind grace stems from the light
of your love that lives in the selfless giving
of yourself to me and my craft. Others fail,
held back by the spring of mutual fear,
and the love they keep locked away they nail
down to the beast which threatens to rear
to the breaking point of hate: the cold war
of the heart which fears the sunburst light
that lies dormant in another. But a far
singing must someday break through the night
of their long darkness, a life's slow death,
to make first contact—the memoried past
which ends brute hatred and stirs the breath
of man and man and man to love at last.

UNIVERSES

We could not see the outside sky—
the billion stars blazing above
the sleeping midnight hours of Wales—
and the far galaxies spinning,
       soundlessly,
              endlessly,
in void upon void upon void
as in still seconds I entered you,
obliterating space, electric-nerved
in the soft collision of body on body,
breaking down advancing barriers
of sleep on sleep where a million
       lovers dream,
              endlessly,
in misty universes of mind and mind
as your slow moan of love
starred a cloud of sound about me
and the flesh cried in a
       blinding light,
              endlessly,
to flare and flash and flame
for miles through our shuttered sky
till meteors blazed alive again
in our island universe of night.

DUELS

The months have worn away
the first keen edge of your desire,
and now you are cool, distant,
when we meet in parties,
or the street.
        You remain 'a friend'.
you say, and yet some razor
feeling in me aches to slake
in you again.
        But your bland words
laugh away my familiar thrusts,
dampen my known fire. I know
that only time can temper me,
hold at bay the smooth glide
of your honed shaft of memory . . .
        Our new partners
are attentive, complacent, unaware
of eyes that spark and clash in
remembered duels—the blades
of our bodies that steel each
other still.
        But you, my love,
are content, knowing the metal
of me now, and you just smile
when we cross and meet and see
each other with another.
        But I strike at you
in silence still—accuse you
as a lost and faithless lover—
and yet I know I am no better.

CEFN COED

They postponed the closure for three months.
They put off for the moment the moment
of final disintegration which begins
with the pit's closure.
                But these few months
are like the numbed space between
death and burial. The rot has begun.
Already the small shops begin to close,
the young drift to the bright lights
of the coastal towns, and family after family
begin to pack for uncertain futures.
                The delaying of death
means nothing. This close community,
this tried culture of stubborn men,
is already dead—and all know it.

THE EASY WAYS

They tell me of the easy ways to live—
of the fat fees paid to poets
        turned copywriters;
of those who seek the safe sanctuary
of broadcasting or academic cloisters.
And they tell of others who live by
        the journalistic knife
which carves up private and public face.

But guilt claws at small talents.
They fool themselves they could
        if they *tried*—
but of course they never get round to it.
And still they hold their genteel parties,
playing out a literary masquerade,
        and talk of poetry as if they,
too, were prisoners of the Muse.

HILL 881

Somewhere in Saigon a general agreed
to let machine-guns sow their barren seed,
and gave the order to attack—
'no turning back,
just take that goddam hill,
and kill and kill and kill and kill!'

The American Marines marched up the hill;
they were young, confused, but eager to kill,
until mortar bombs blew them back again
to leave them shrieking in shattered pain.

Somewhere in Hanoi a general agreed
to slaughter peasants caged by a creed,
and gave the order to counter-attack—
'No turning back,
we must hold that hill,
and kill and kill and kill and kill!'

The North Vietnamese marched down the hill;
they were young, confused, driven to kill,
until the napalm splattered like fiery rain
and the B52s blew them apart again.

Then far from war we watch the news, turn away,
shrugging, saying it will end one day—
while in that same moment of time,
young men in their prime,
blindly battle for a bloody, useless hill,
and kill and kill and kill and kill!